All Those Lilting Tongues

poems by

Theresa Hamman

Finishing Line Press
Georgetown, Kentucky

All Those Lilting Tongues

Copyright © 2018 by Theresa Hamman
ISBN 978-1-63534-685-5 First Edition
All rights reserved under International and Pan-American Copyright Conventions.
No part of this book may be reproduced in any manner whatsoever without written permission from the publisher, except in the case of brief quotations embodied in critical articles and reviews.

ACKNOWLEDGMENTS

Poems previously published from this collection include the following:

"Aftermath: Divorce Finalized" and "What Was Breaking" in *Nailed Magazine*
"Absorption," "Rain" and "Love is Suicide" in *Oregon East*
"Without" and "Rebirth" in *Red Savina Review*
"All Hues," "I Missed You Dying" and "The Day My Father Died" in *The Tower Journal*
"Pretty Flames All in a Row" and "It's a Waste of Magic to Wish Someone Dead" in *basalt*
"Driving the Desert with Zep" in *The Paddock Review*

Publisher: Leah Maines
Editor: Christen Kincaid
Cover Art: Stefano Imbert
Author Photo: Theresa Hamman
Cover Design: Elizabeth Maines McCleavy

Printed in the USA on acid-free paper.
Order online: www.finishinglinepress.com
also available on amazon.com

Author inquiries and mail orders:
Finishing Line Press
P. O. Box 1626
Georgetown, Kentucky 40324
U. S. A.

Table of Contents

The Day My Father Died 1

All Hues 2

Love Is Suicide 3

What Was Breaking 4

Aftermath: Divorce Finalized 6

I Missed You Dying 7

Without 8

And It All Means 9

Rebirth 10

Pretty Flames All in a Row 11

It's a Waste of Magic to Wish Someone Dead 13

Rain 17

Absorption 18

Memory Charms Fall 19

What I Feel Like Doing 20

Winter People 21

Driving the Desert with Zep 23

For my mother, Mary:
"What hat are you wearing today?"

For my daughters, Bethany and Mara:
"This is the song that never ends, it goes on and on..."

For my grandchildren, Savannah and Steven:
"Go where-ever dreaming goes"

And for my father, Benny:
"Papa, watch me fly"

The Day My Father Died

I roamed the cemetery
searching for the best
place, one with a view

of autumn on the mountain
as if he would see
the fall, the impending snow.

I saw him watching
the spring green up
with his neighbors

as if they all shared
the same ladder,
lifting open each other's doors

and climbing out
in the morning, igniting
each other's eyes with suns.

All Hues

I miss the early us when
we were in our grass roots.

The way we laughed in summer
at picnics before we fell
out of each other.

Between the hush and glass
against winter along a fence
white over white
rails of barb-blanched wood.

Inside, the room sighs dust.
The portrait of us on a leafy limb
lands without holding hands.

The baby grand in the parlor
upholds its tuning, sings its reds and browns
before all this whiting.

Love Is Suicide

It begins with a beating and
results in deep wounds
needing to be stitched.
She shows him how the last
of her is bleeding out,
how inadequate
        her hands are.

But he
won't stay with her,
or go back to her,
or wash away the nightmare
he used to bash her.
He only tells her love
is suicide, and she
holds the note
        he wrote all over her body.

What Was Breaking

She sees herself,
her husband
in the living room
holding each other on the couch.

The bookshelves,
half full,
the television glowing
in the midnight dark,
the baby pressed
to her breast.

A moment stuck
in its own happiness,
false, fragile,
a moment belonging
to a hope long lost.

She can't stand it.

She blinks,
the image blurs,
rain on glass.

It clears.

And the beer can explodes
against the kitchen wall,
directly above the baby,
who chews on cheerios
in her high chair.
Beer rains down
the baby laughs.

"Look, she likes it,"
her husband says.
"She's sucking it off her thumb."

Aftermath: Divorce Finalized

A neighbor's truck
ignited for no reason.
Sparks jumped and lit the dead
Eucalyptus in my front yard.
I watched from the window. Firemen
arrived, doused both truck and tree.

Fire is a rain dance
and I sighed as the flames died.
One fireman asked if I was the lady
who called 911.

"It was never me."

The next day, I loaded up
the Cutlass with clothes, trinkets, cats
and babies. I locked
the front door. Then I stood
for a moment and stared
at the tree's charred remains.
My neighbor ran
over and apologized, his truck
had never done anything like that before.

I Missed You Dying

because you were
going all along

because I never thought
you would allow such endings

staying so wide awake
under the silver IV tree

with its sound drip
its leafless arms

on that day
the veins went dry

and I stayed away
because no radiance

survives such silence.

I could not bear your unlit gaze.

Without

> *Remembered happiness is agony;*
> *So is remembered agony.*
> *~Donald Hall*

Tell me again
how grief waters
the iris of an eye.

Remind me how
to walk this shore without
your hand
or your skin warm
beneath your coat.

I no longer hear you
sing ice
over this sea.

Show me again the way
your hair fell white
covering your eyes.

My callings
go unanswered

and the sunset
has lost your name.

And It All Means

We crawl along the Earth's spine, listen for the whirr
and whine of engines revving up for flight, hoping for a way

off. It's a black dawn and the oily dew shimmers. Sap
clings to our dead-log bodies while we ache for the breaking

point when our lungs can finally implode, when our claws
can chisel out the Tree's heart, when our fleas can bite past skin into bone.

And it all means termites, or rust, or seepage, or maybe—

just maybe

a chance to be nothing more than waste,
nothing more than regurgitated paradise.

Rebirth

a fracture
one dead eye
perched on a high
cliff watches

the plates shift.

Beyond,
you hear the way
the river glops over
an orange cascade,
weighty, dense, and

you carry
skins of rain
collected long before fires,
before all that acid,
and feel

the way your back
fissures open

blisters—

oiling out
all black

creating new rivers.

Pretty Flames All in a Row

This is
a morning sick
with hangover
and rain
after everything
is all dried up.
It tinks
on the bottles left
on the patio
table, the thirst
is appalling, but
the lightning is
so showy. how
it slices
through a jet stream
smeared with dye.

You become
the throaty drawl
in my head
no pill
can silence.
You pulsate
my brain,
you swizzle
the lining of my
stomach.

On the TV
a news report:
a blood-smeared
Harley in a driveway.
Who did it murder?

By the way—

What ever happened
to the crazy dogs
who rode the hogs
and howled at tinny radios?

Ah well, never mind—

The long noon nap stretches
toward evening and then evening
eases into night like a sleepy cat.
The way out
opens to dark matter;
a Fat Boy thunders by, it's stirring
up a waste of gold dust,
a treasure
I hold in my bones.

Where's the lightning?

Ah, there—

All neon flashy
over the entrance
of Clyde's Biker Bar,
the hogs lined up,
pretty flames all in a row.

It's a Waste of Magic to Wish Someone Dead

1.

Now that the house is painted,
and the mountain is swathed in autumn,
and before the fisherman's hat
is frozen in the lake, it's time
to get a new cushion for the window seat.

2.

The woman says the hoses are on the roof
to keep them out of the reach of children.
Consider how odd it is
that children are always crying in parking lots.

3.

It's a waste of magic to wish someone dead.

4.

The portal through shadows
is as long as the gloaming forest's
row of trees.
The sparks from the cabin's hearth
offer only candle-stick illumination.
The keyhole is shut, but the coffee
is percolating. A marshmallow
fell into the fire and grew into a cloud.

5.

Never mind the indigo
tear drop on the doll,
the paint faded years ago,
the hands that held her
are now manicured with fake nails.

6.

Consider this robin,
she comes to the cherries,
then flies away to some other
sweetness when they are all devoured.

7.

The new cushion for the window seat
needs to be therapeutic. My mother
watches the birth of snowmen
through frosted glass.

8.

Consider this unraveling sweater,
Its wool is cheap, comes from underfed
sheep, whose herder's dollar never
comes back to his hand. Wearing it
to the pumpkin patch on Sunday
is risky, its pockets are gone by noon.

9.

The lucky people are the ones who
not only win the weekly shoe lotteries, but
also the annual lottery of socks.

10.

The stories I'm telling are all
based on truth. Expiration
dates get in the way,
and the dates in the apple
bowl are shriveled
but still sweet.

11.

It's idiotic to run from ghosts.

12.

Listen—
the ghosts are trying
to say you are not dead.

13.

Do you think the moon abhors us?

14.

Back to the seat cushion,
the window's view of the
tulips as they erupt
is a checker board. The beams
cross-stitch a pattern
of bells that ring
at each intersection.

Rain

The least of us stand in long lines
waiting to go out in the rain. We
watch and blame the door
for its narrowness.
Lesser still the way we seek lightning
and thunder
sounding some signal
that the sky exists. Looking up
makes no difference, the door remains
itself, gaping open, allowing
for only a small percent
of the masses to exit.

Absorption

Cast me over mud.

Be sure
to avoid the stepping stones,
the creek banks,
the back yard
Azaleas. Absorption requires
deep, wet loam.

Cast me wide,
with an arcing swing,
on a day with no wind.

Memory Charms Fall

from an elderly
bracelet they tumble
like crystal balls
across hardwood
floors, cartwheel through
doors and down
back halls,

calling themselves
finer hours, grand
intentions laid out
when the days began,
before the fall of years,
before the fall of the last bed.

What I Feel Like Doing

Honestly?

I don't know
what I feel like doing
all these places
don't open until nine.

I thought

Fall would brighten
the wilting greens
with its air
full of roasted corn
and leaves
and chimneys roaring
to life.

But the days
are the same
with their long lag
and even longer tails.

I thought
once the smoke cleared
and the rains came
the hours would become

friendly

and I could talk to them
or sing their lyrics
while doing laundry
but the words are stale
having baked too long
under summer's jaundice sun.

Winter People

> *The way a crow*
> *Shook down on me*
> *The dust of snow*
> *From a hemlock tree*
> *~Robert Frost, Dust of Snow*

i

    it's cold

the way the floor
stretches our children
into stains of smeared ice
cream that melt
and refreeze
all pink and brown,

the way their sticky
shoes leave prints,
as though they hope
to one day follow
their feet home.

ii

    what is

"I'm sorry"
to me now?
after all
this floor, these walls
know only the way

    your blizzards hang
    off the over
    coats in the yard.

iii

        all you

ever do
is show me
how your subzero
lips curl
around your canary
teeth
as you gnaw
on an old steak bone.

iv.

        in late afternoon

I listen
to the sing-song
voices of our children
chanting Frost

        a crow shook down on me

while they press pieces
of stained glass
into balls of snow
to make
their winter people smile.

Driving the Desert with Zep

We were bees once in May
before the lilac blooms blew
away, before we were itchy,
always scratching and eating
prickly pears while our skin peeled
and twisted inside out. We kissed

before our chapped lips cracked
from all that thirsty August heat,
before we rolled naked into cactus
water and wrapped ourselves in snake
skin, before we laughed

while the yellow desert ate us,
and its hornet's nest erupted
into "Kashmir" and all that floating
dust, all those lilting tongues—

found us.

Do you remember?

We knew how to buzz once,
how to light up
before we became dead jackets,
before we became sulfured honey.

Theresa Hamman is a poet who lives in La Grande, Oregon. Born in 1963 in Michigan, she moved with her family to Arizona when she was nine years-old. Unable to cope with the Arizona heat, she and her two daughters relocated to a small rural northeast Oregon town called John Day in 1998. Five years later, in 2004, she and her daughters moved to La Grande. In 2011, after being laid off from her small office assistant job, she decided to attend Eastern Oregon University to earn her Master of Fine Arts in poetry degree. She graduated in 2016. She is currently in the process of earning her Master of Arts degree in English Literature at Mercy College in New York.

Theresa also teaches undergraduate composition and creative writing courses at Eastern Oregon University and Southern New Hampshire University as a part time adjunct professor.

Her poems can be found in the following: *The Tower Journal, Oregon East, basalt, The Paddock Review, Red Savina Review* and *Nailed*.

Although Theresa enjoys writing in all creative genres, her first love is poetry. She gets lost in its musicality and enjoys how it bends language to create new objects.

All Those Lilting Tongues is her first poetry chapbook collection.

www.ingramcontent.com/pod-product-compliance
Lightning Source LLC
LaVergne TN
LVHW041518070426
835507LV00012B/1670